# Wolf Spiders

by Claire Archer

**www.abdopublishing.com**

Published by Abdo Kids, a division of ABDO, PO Box 398166, Minneapolis, Minnesota 55439.

Copyright © 2015 by Abdo Consulting Group, Inc. International copyrights reserved in all countries. No part of this book may be reproduced in any form without written permission from the publisher.

Printed in the United States of America, North Mankato, Minnesota.

052014

092014

Photo Credits: Shutterstock, Thinkstock

Production Contributors: Teddy Borth, Jennie Forsberg, Grace Hansen

Design Contributors: Candice Keimig, Laura Rask, Dorothy Toth


Library of Congress Control Number: 2013952996

Cataloging-in-Publication Data

Archer, Claire.

 Wolf spiders / Claire Archer.

  p. cm. -- (Spiders)

ISBN 978-1-62970-076-2 (lib. bdg.)

Includes bibliographical references and index.

1. Wolf spiders--Juvenile literature.   I. Title.

595.4--dc23

                    2013952996

# Table of Contents

## Wolf Spiders

Wolf spiders live around the world. They usually live in grasslands and meadows.

Wolf spiders come in a few colors. Most are brown, black, gray, or tan.

Wolf spiders have **markings** on their bodies. They usually have stripes.

8

Wolf spiders have eight eyes.

They have excellent eyesight.

## Hunting

Wolf spiders can see very well at night. They hunt mostly at night.

13

A wolf spider stalks its prey. Then it pounces. It rolls onto its back. It holds the prey with its legs.

The wolf spider then bites its **prey**. It injects its prey with **venom**.

## Baby Wolf Spiders

Female wolf spiders wrap their eggs in silk. They carry their eggs under their **abdomens**.

The baby spiders hatch.
The mother carries them
for weeks. Then they are
ready to live on their own.

21

# More Facts

- Wolf spiders are the only spiders that carry their young on their backs.

- Wolf spiders are not very big. Most only grow to be just over 1 inch (2.54 cm) long. This does not include the length of their legs, however.

- Female wolf spiders are usually larger than males.

- Wolf spiders mostly eat insects and other spiders.

# Glossary

**abdomen** – the back part of a spider's body.

**markings** – a mark or pattern of marks on an animal's fur, feathers, or skin.

**pounce** – to spring or jump suddenly.

**prey** – an animal hunted or killed for food.

**stalk** – to secretly follow prey.

**venom** – a poison made by some animals.

# Index

## abdokids.com

Use this code to log on to abdokids.com and access crafts, games, videos and more!

Abdo Kids Code:

**SWK0762**